ROCK GUITAR FOR KIDS SONGBOOK

MW00582162

ISBN 0-7935-9998-9

HAL•LEONARD®
CORPORATION
7777 W. BLUEMOUND RD. P.O. BOX 13819 MILWAUKEE, WI 53213

Visit Hal Leonard Online at
www.halleonard.com

Contents

Introduction

Welcome to the **Rock Guitar for Kids Songbook**—a collection of eight great songs by your favorite rock artists, complete with play-along CD!

This book is intended as a companion to **Beginning Rock Guitar for Kids**, a fun, easy introduction to playing guitar that's oriented towards **today's** kid. If you've complete that book, you already know the basics of rock guitar—including how to read music and TAB, how to play power chords and riffs, and how to start jamming on some simple rhythm and lead patterns. This songbook will take your playing even further, as you learn complete songs by artists like the Kinks, Van Halen, Nirvana, the Offspring, Sublime, No Doubt, and more. (If you don't have **Beginning Rock Guitar for Kids** but still know most of the basics, you'll do just fine!)

Before we begin, a word of warning: many of the songs in this book contain chords, rhythms, and techniques that will be new to you. Don't get discouraged! The accompanying CD should help you out. The CD features every song recorded by a **full** band so you can hear how each song sounds, and play along when you're ready.

Remember: playing guitar should be fun. However, to become a good guitarist, you have to practice regularly. Keep in mind that it's better to practice for just a few minutes a day than to cram all your practicing into one long session once or twice per week. Try to stick to a regular practice schedule, but don't feel bad if you miss a day every now and then. Go at your own pace, and enjoy yourself!

About the CD

Playing along with the accompanying CD will give you practice in playing with a full band—plus it's fun. Each song is preceded by one measure of "clicks" to indicate the tempo and meter. Pan right to hear the guitar part emphasized. Pan left to hear the rest of the band emphasized.

◆ Wild Thing

Words and Music by
CHIP TAYLOR

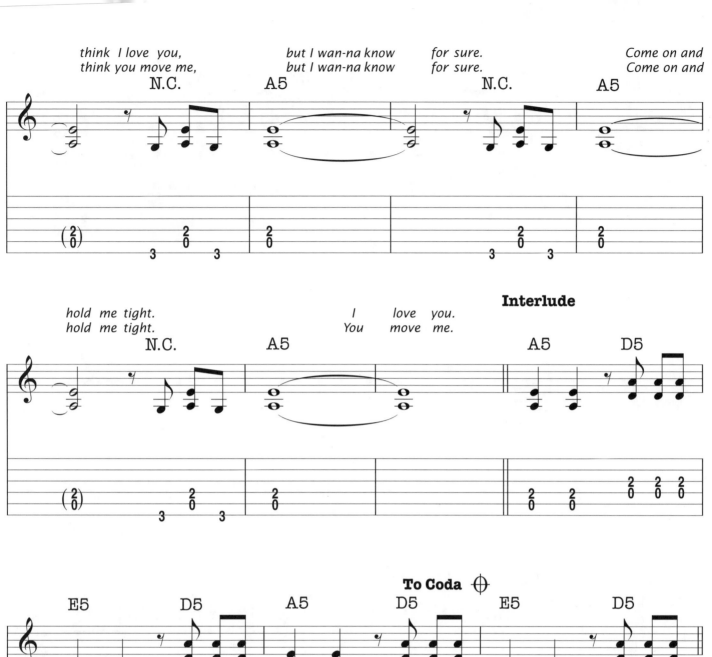

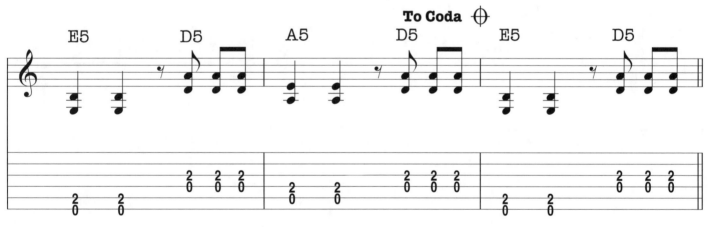

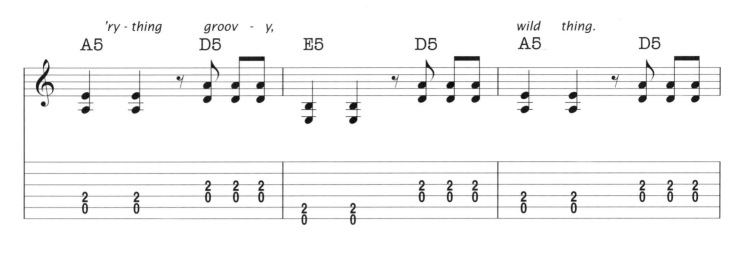

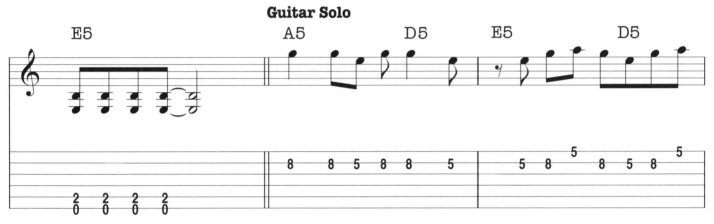

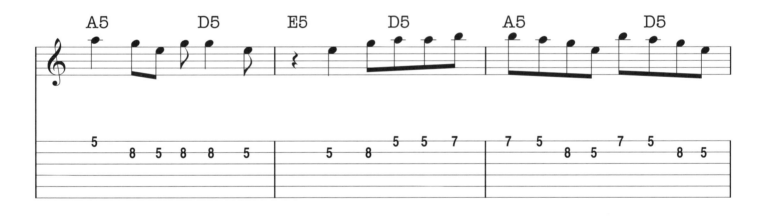

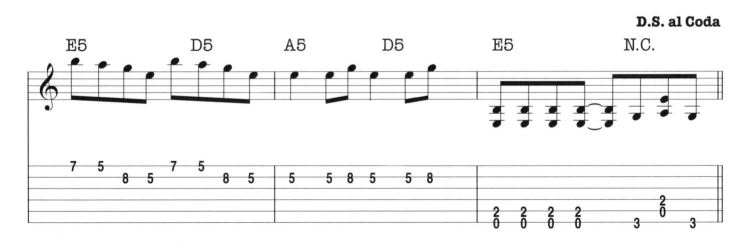

② You Really Got Me

Words and Music by
RAY DAVIES

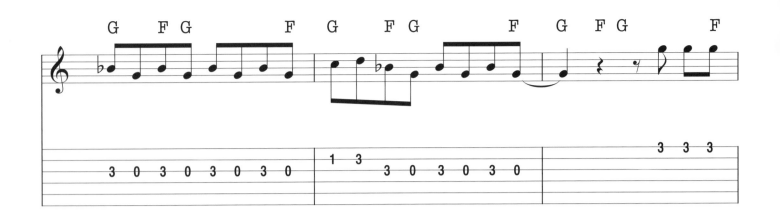

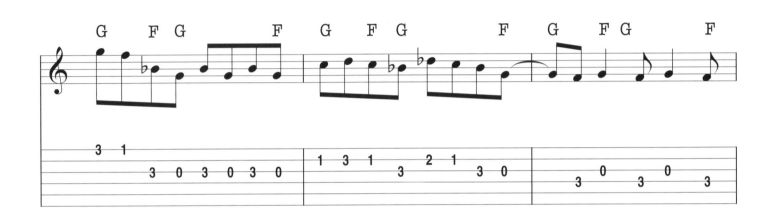

D.S. al Coda

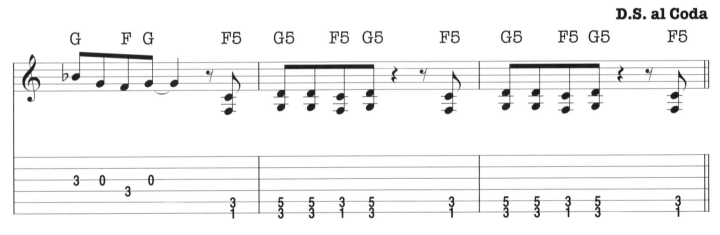

3 Tubthumping

Words and Music by NIGEL HUNTER, BRUCE DUNCAN,
ALICE NUTTER, LOUISE WATTS, PAUL GRECO,
DARREN HAMER, ALLEN WHALLEY and JUDITH ABBOTT

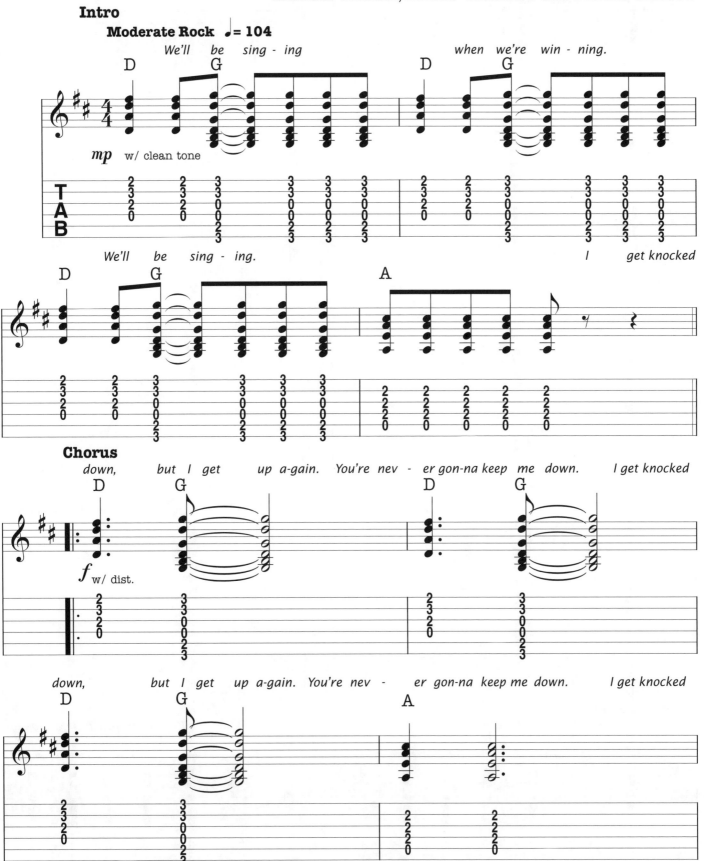

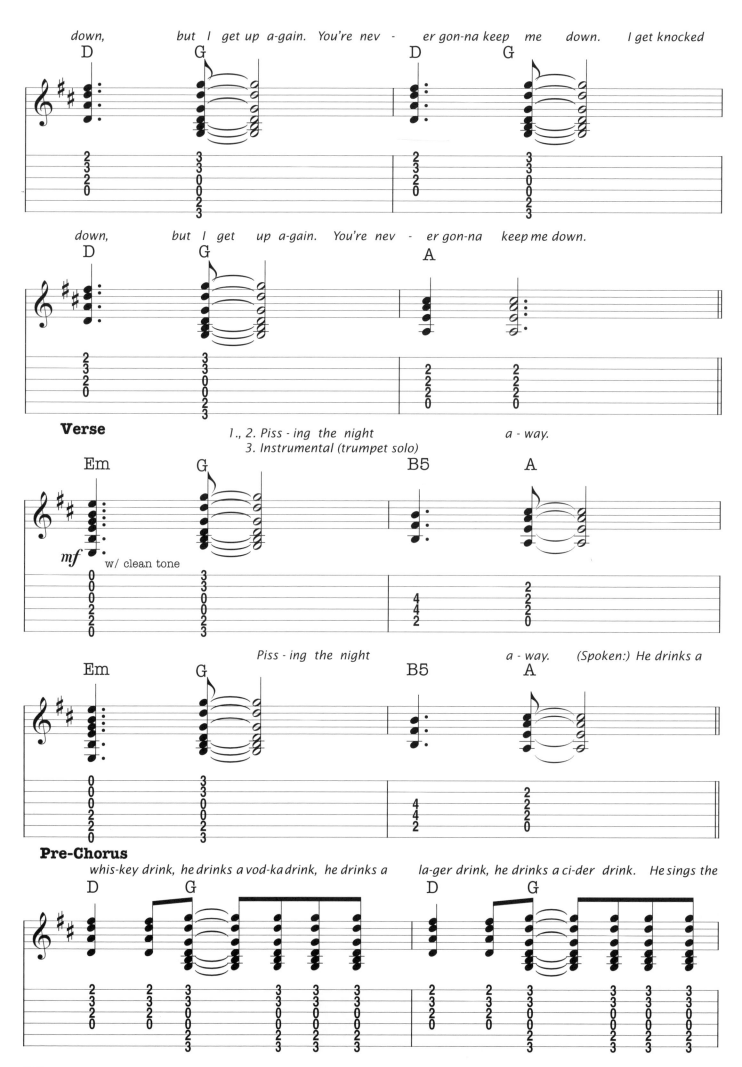

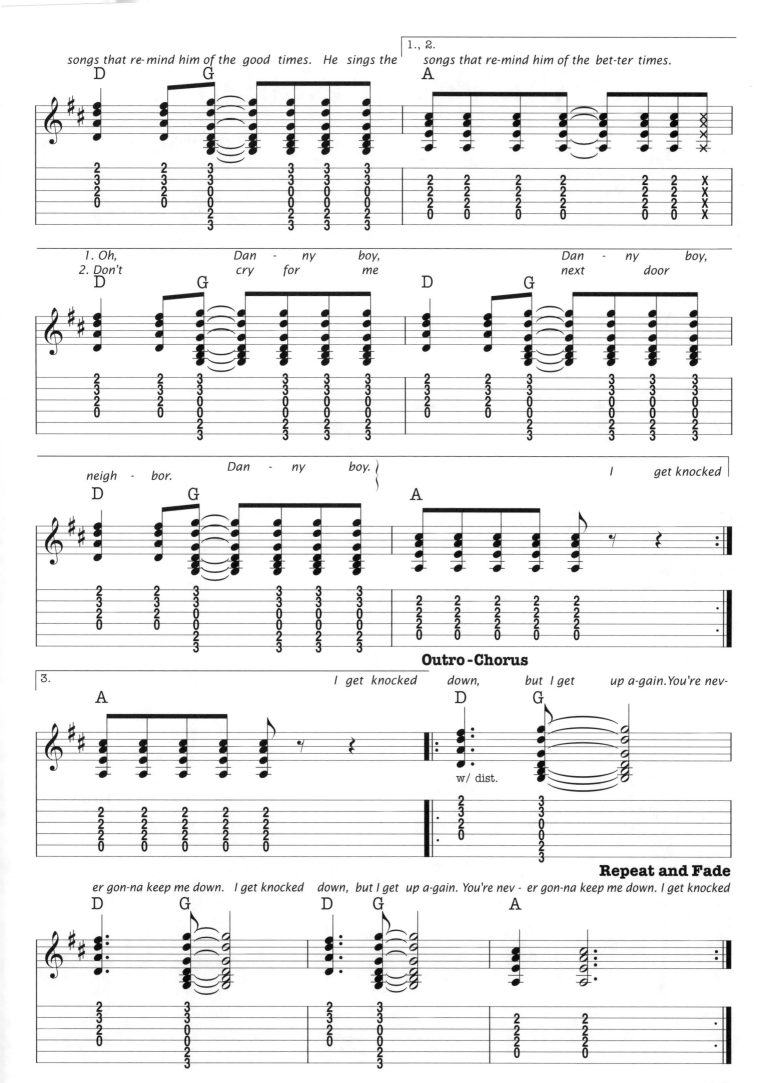

◆ Oh, Pretty Woman

Words and Music by
ROY ORBISON and BILL DEES

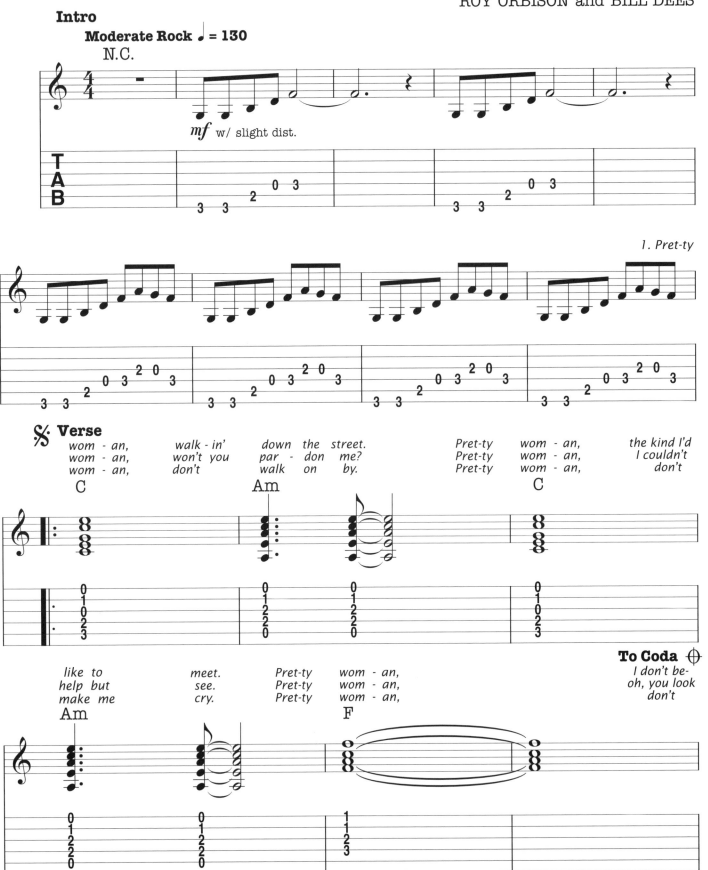

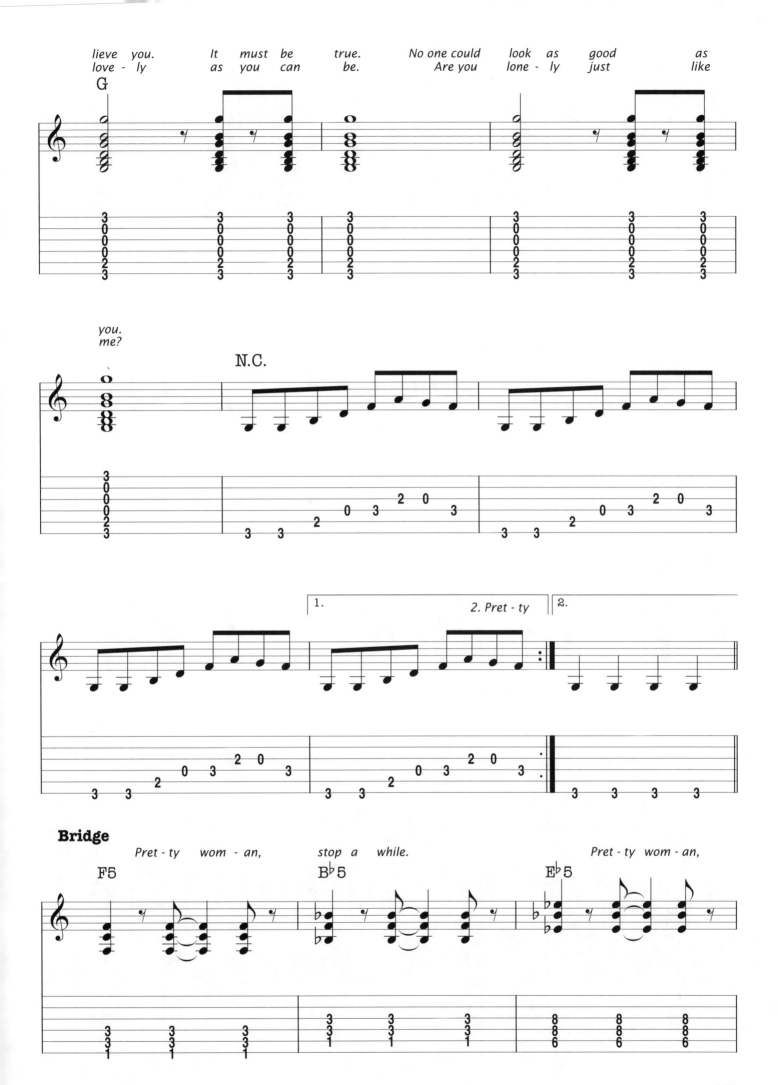

16

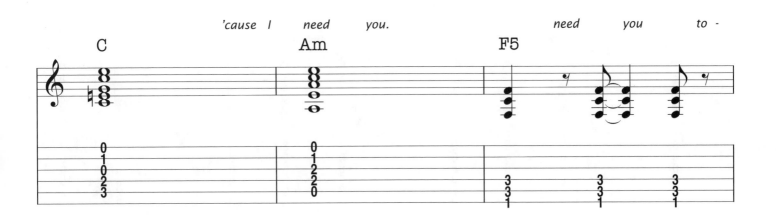

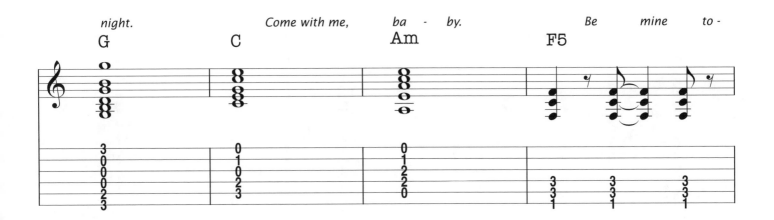

D.S. al Coda

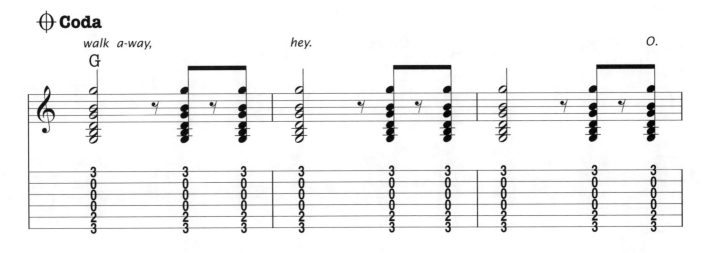

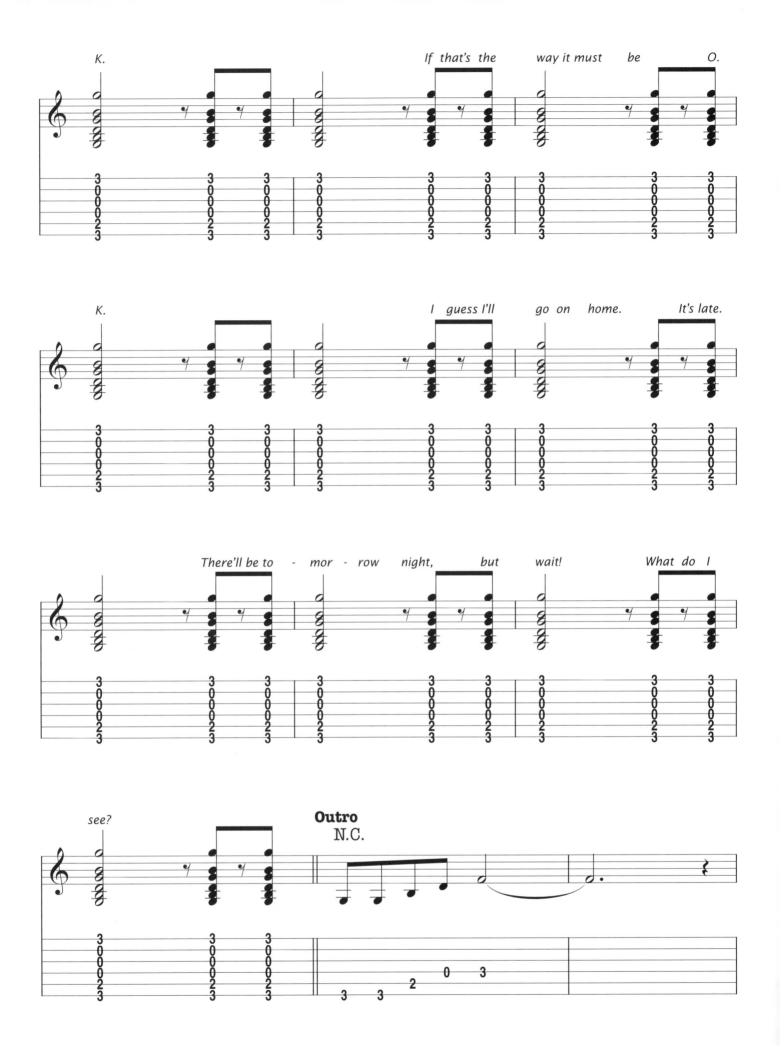

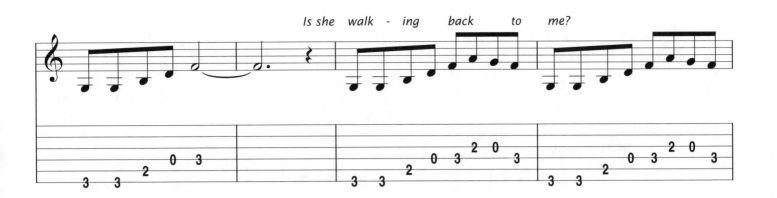

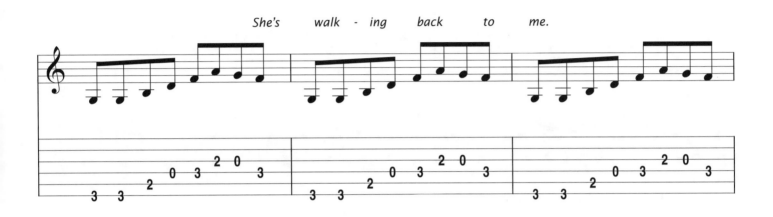

◆The Man Who Sold the World

Words and Music by
DAVID BOWIE

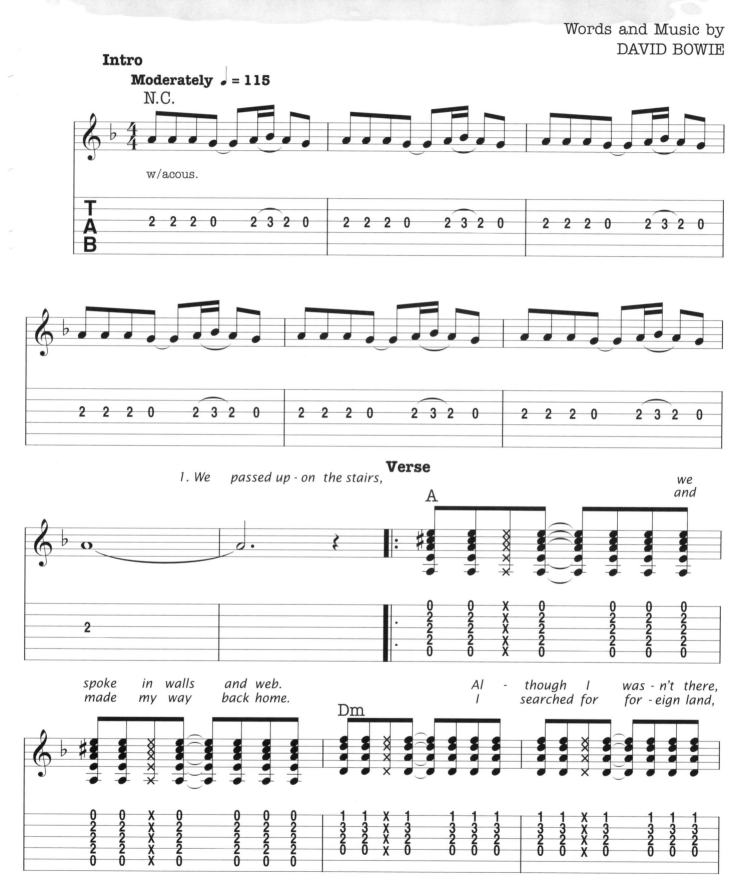

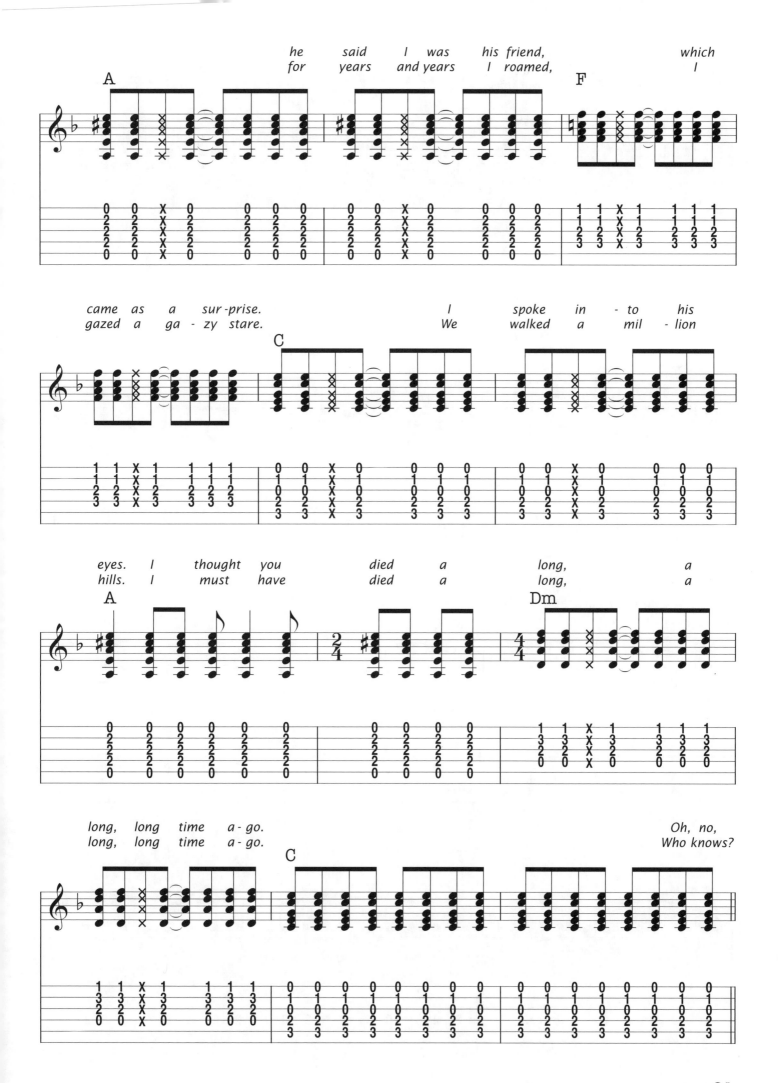

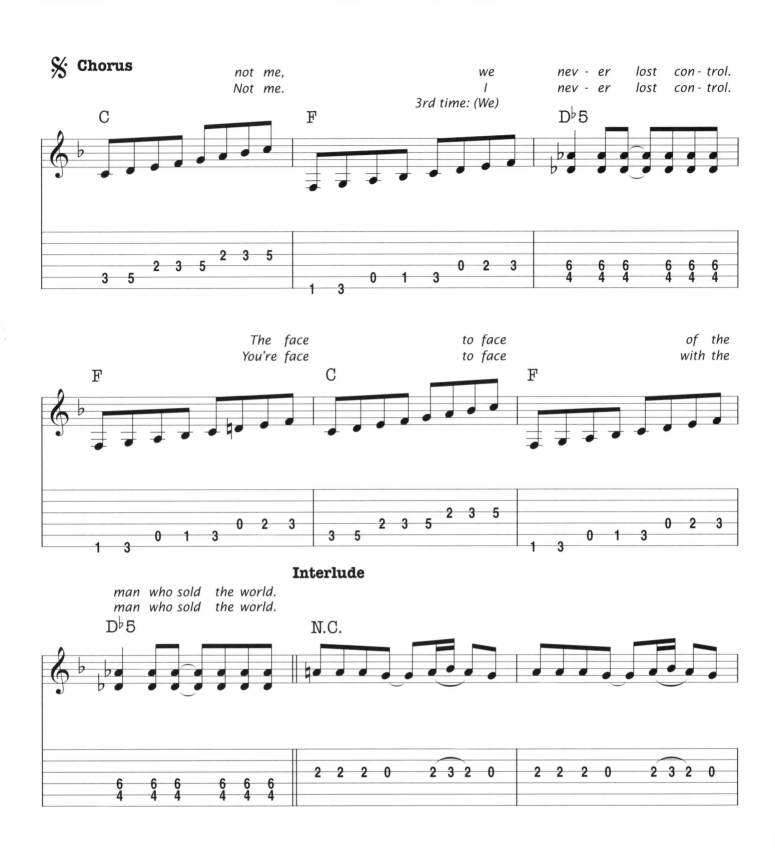

Interlude

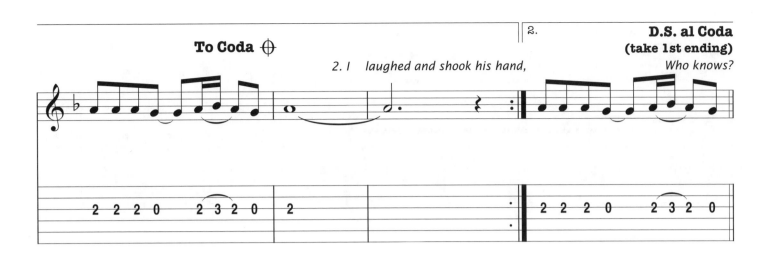

To Coda ⊕

2. I laughed and shook his hand,

D.S. al Coda
(take 1st ending)

Who knows?

2.

⊕ **Coda**
Outro–Guitar Solo

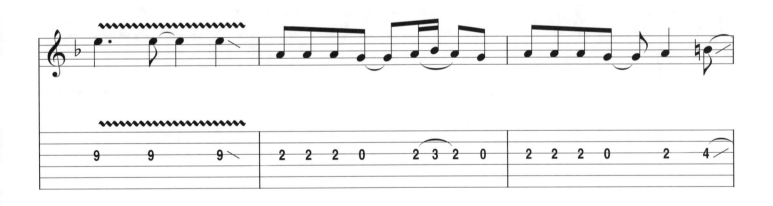

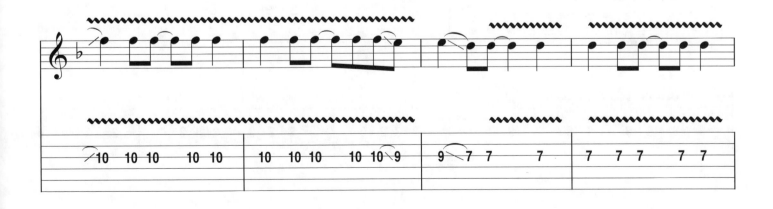

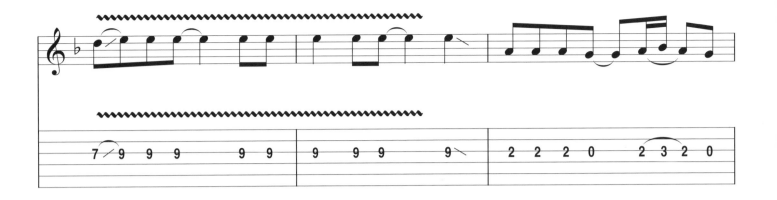

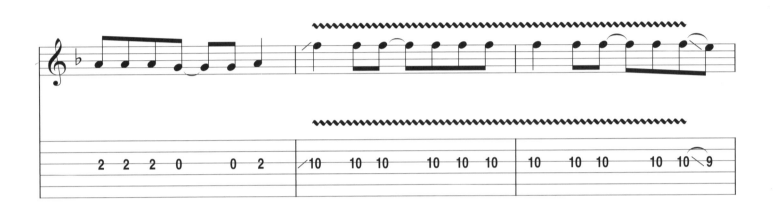

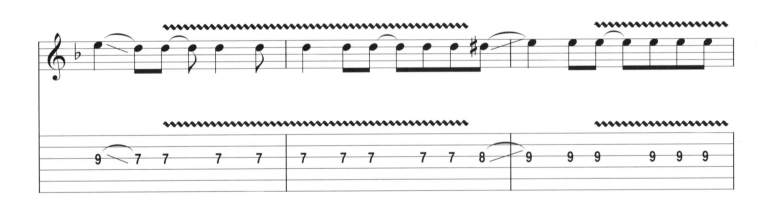

◆ Come Out and Play

Words and Music by
DEXTER HOLLAND

Intro

Moderate Rock ♩ = 160

You got-ta keep 'em sep-a-rat-ed.

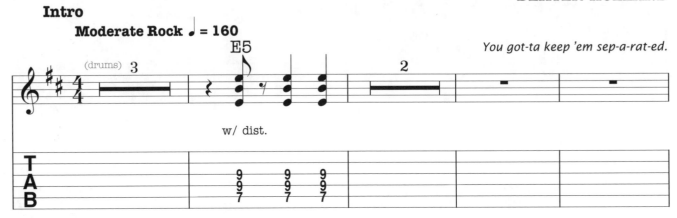

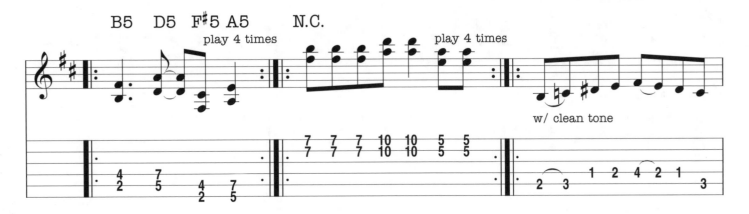

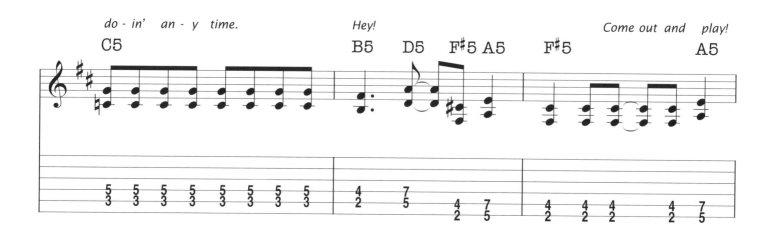

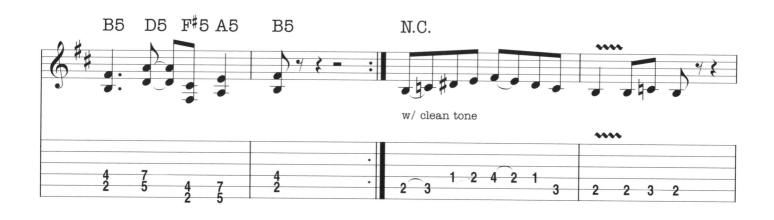

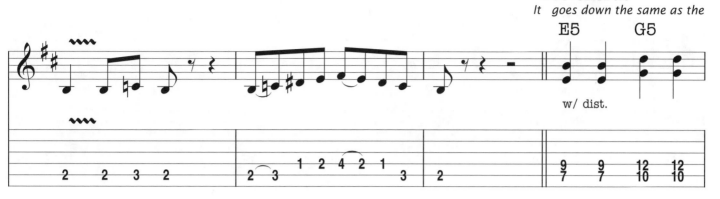
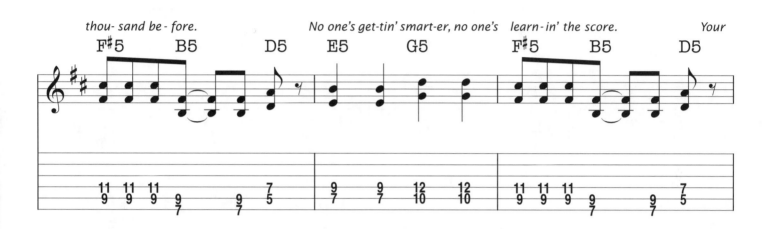
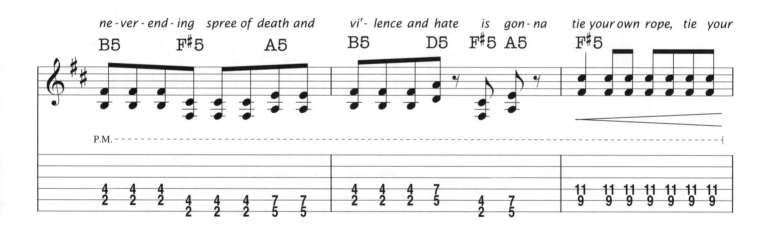

Chorus

◆ What I Got

Words and Music by BRAD NOWELL,
ERIC WILSON and FLOYD GAUGH

Intro

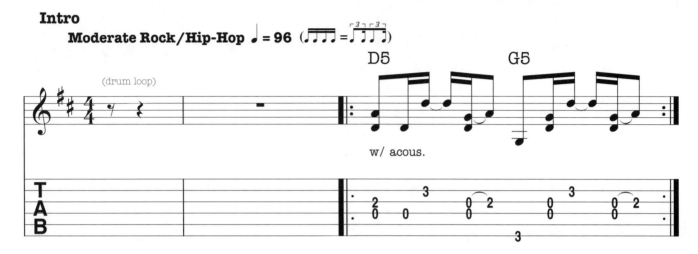

 Verse

1. Ear - ly   in   the morn - ing   ris - in'   to   the street.   Light
2. is, so love the one you got...
3. Why I don't cry when my dog runs a-way...

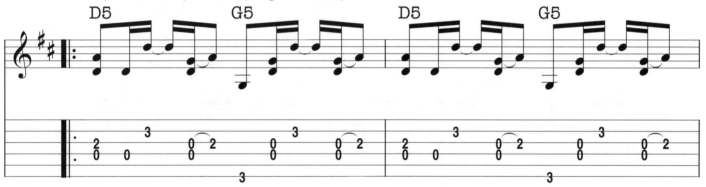

me   up   that cig - a - rette and I'll   strap shoes on   my   feet.

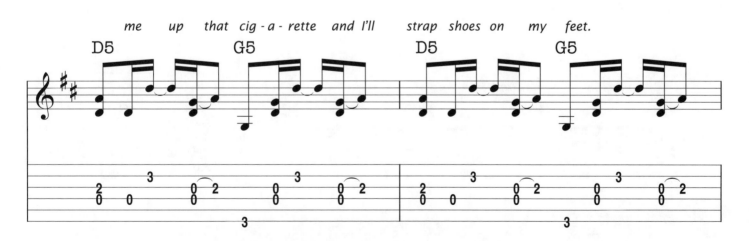

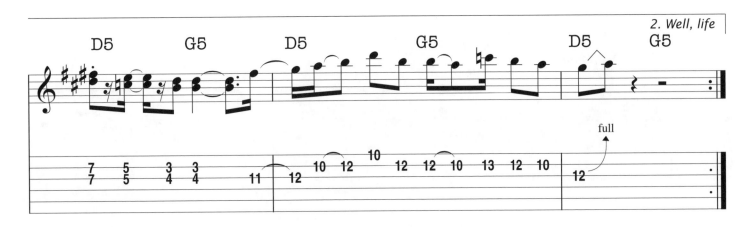

2.

Chorus

Lov-in'   is what I got,   I said re-mem-ber that.   Lov - in'   is what I got

and re-mem-ber that. Lov - in'   is what I got,   I said re-mem-ber that.

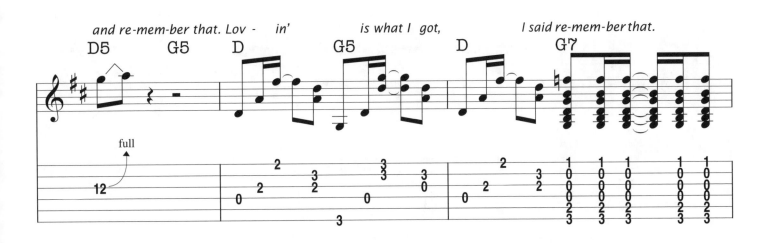

D.S. al Coda

Lov - in'   is what I got,   I got, I got, I   got.

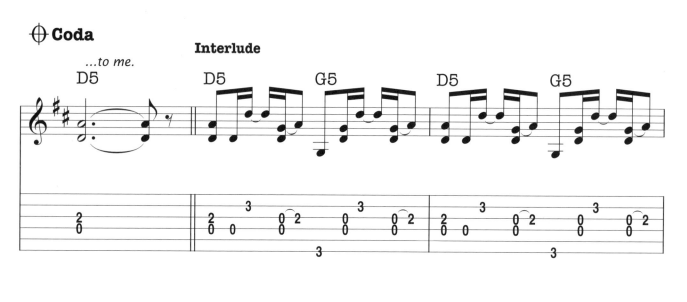

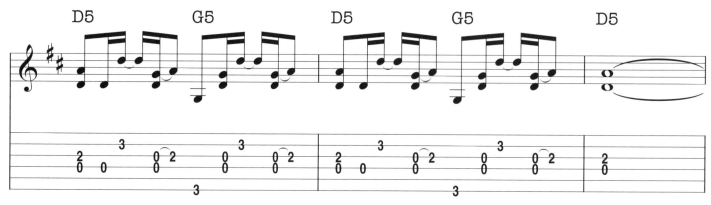

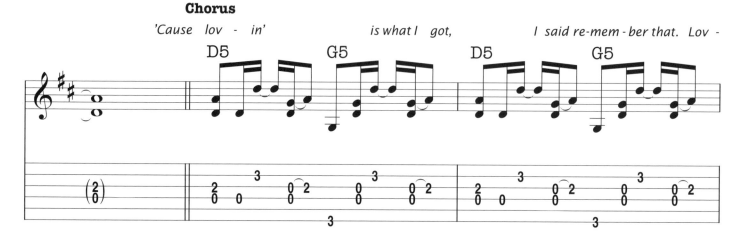

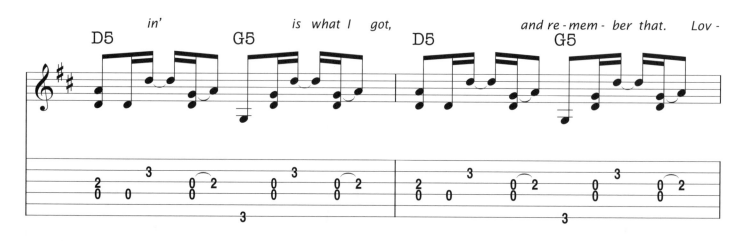

◆ Just a Girl

Words and Music by
GWEN STEFANI and THOMAS DUMONT

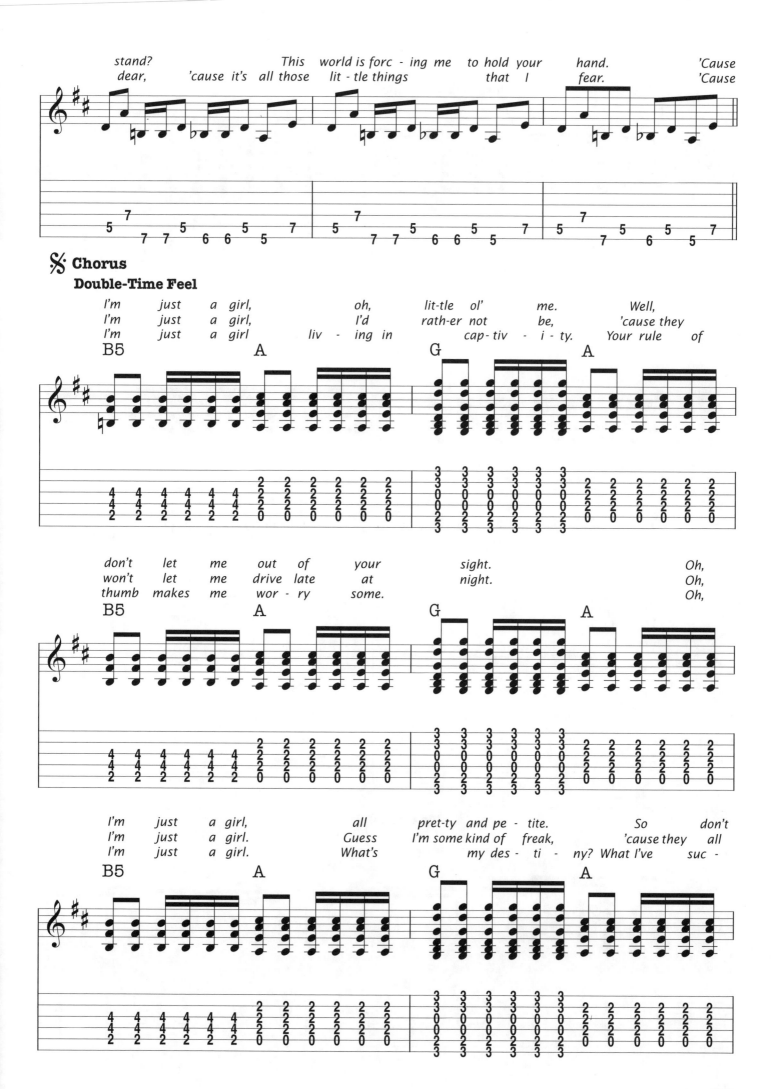

Chorus
Double-Time Feel

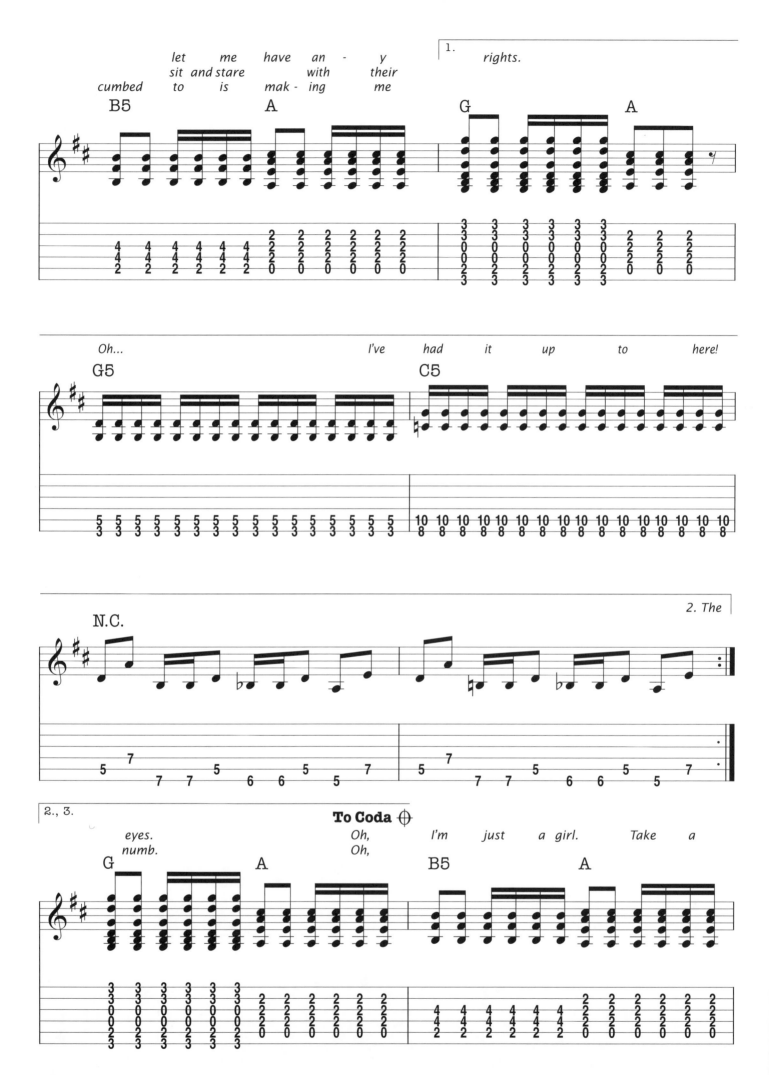

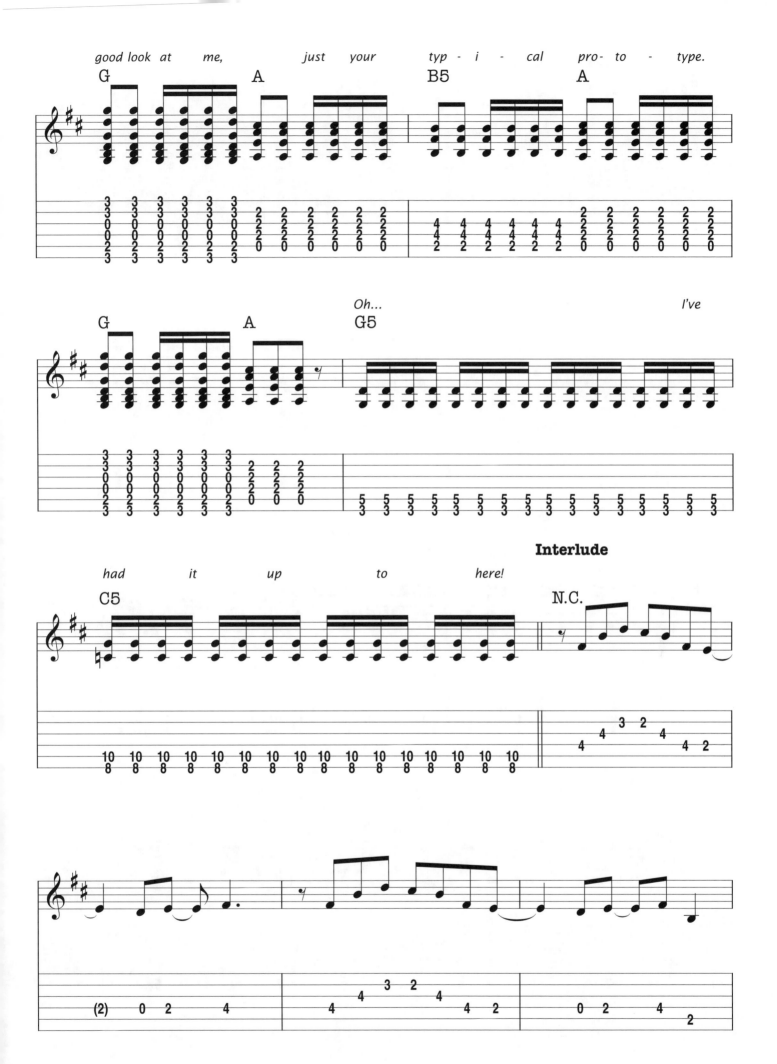

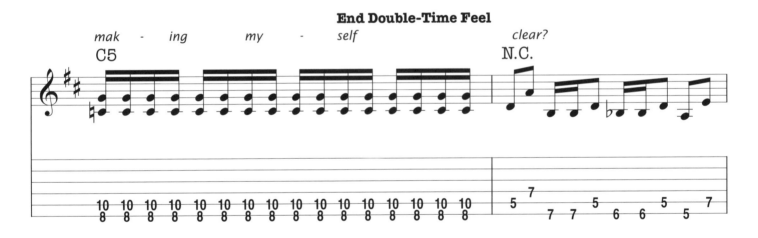

End Double-Time Feel

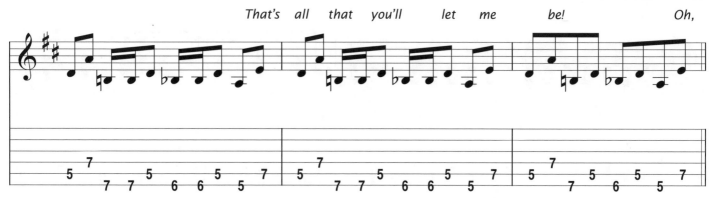

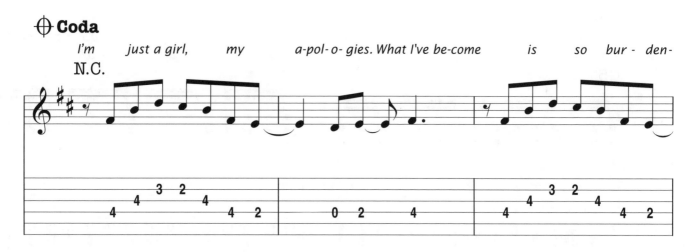

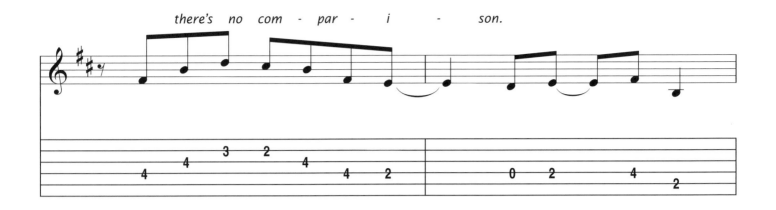

there's no com - par - i - son.

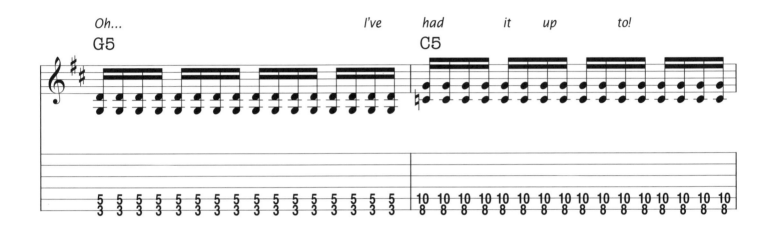

Oh...   I've   had   it   up   to!

G5   C5

Oh...   I've   had   it   up   to!!

G5   C5

End Double-Time Feel

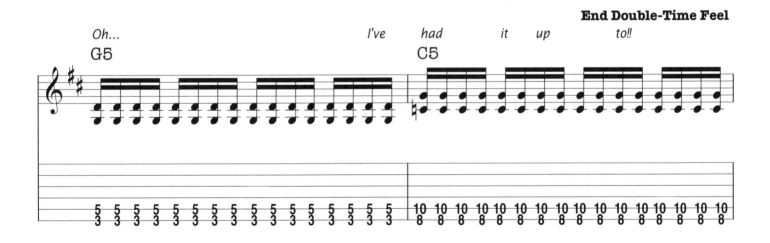

Slower ♩ = 92   **Freely**

Oh...   I've had it up   to   here.

G5   C5   B5

rit.

Guitar Notation Legend

Guitar Music can be notated three different ways: on a *musical staff*, in *tablature*, and in *rhythm slashes*.

RHYTHM SLASHES are written above the staff. Strum chords in the rhythm indicated. Use the chord diagrams found at the top of the first page of the transcription for the appropriate chord voicings. Round noteheads indicate single notes.

THE MUSICAL STAFF shows pitches and rhythms and is divided by bar lines into measures. Pitches are named after the first seven letters of the alphabet.

TABLATURE graphically represents the guitar fingerboard. Each horizontal line represents a a string, and each number represents a fret.

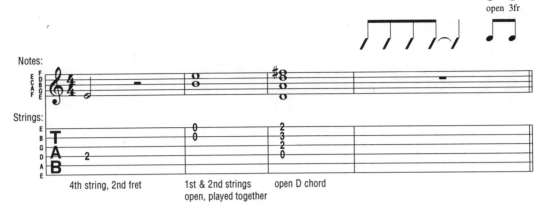

4th string, 2nd fret

1st & 2nd strings open, played together

open D chord

Definitions for Special Guitar Notation

HALF-STEP BEND: Strike the note and bend up 1/2 step.

WHOLE-STEP BEND: Strike the note and bend up one step.

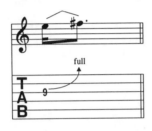

GRACE NOTE BEND: Strike the note and bend up as indicated. The first note does not take up any time.

SLIGHT (MICROTONE) BEND: Strike the note and bend up 1/4 step.

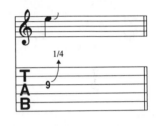

BEND AND RELEASE: Strike the note and bend up as indicated, then release back to the original note. Only the first note is struck.

PRE-BEND: Bend the note as indicated, then strike it.

PRE-BEND AND RELEASE: Bend the note as indicated. Strike it and release the bend back to the original note.

UNISON BEND: Strike the two notes simultaneously and bend the lower note up to the pitch of the higher.

VIBRATO: The string is vibrated by rapidly bending and releasing the note with the fretting hand.

WIDE VIBRATO: The pitch is varied to a greater degree by vibrating with the fretting hand.

HAMMER-ON: Strike the first (lower) note with one finger, then sound the higher note (on the same string) with another finger by fretting it without picking.

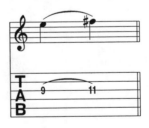

PULL-OFF: Place both fingers on the notes to be sounded. Strike the first note and without picking, pull the finger off to sound the second (lower) note.

LEGATO SLIDE: Strike the first note and then slide the same fret-hand finger up or down to the second note. The second note is not struck.

SHIFT SLIDE: Same as legato slide, except the second note is struck.

TRILL: Very rapidly alternate between the notes indicated by continuously hammering on and pulling off.

TAPPING: Hammer ("tap") the fret indicated with the pick-hand index or middle finger and pull off to the note fretted by the fret hand.

NATURAL HARMONIC: Strike the note while the fret-hand lightly touches the string directly over the fret indicated.

PINCH HARMONIC: The note is fretted normally and a harmonic is produced by adding the edge of the thumb or the tip of the index finger of the pick hand to the normal pick attack.

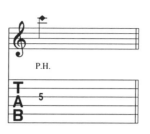

HARP HARMONIC: The note is fretted normally and a harmonic is produced by gently resting the pick hand's index finger directly above the indicated fret (in parentheses) while the pick hand's thumb or pick assists by plucking the appropriate string.

PICK SCRAPE: The edge of the pick is rubbed down (or up) the string, producing a scratchy sound.

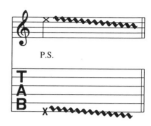

MUFFLED STRINGS: A percussive sound is produced by laying the fret hand across the string(s) without depressing, and striking them with the pick hand.

PALM MUTING: The note is partially muted by the pick hand lightly touching the string(s) just before the bridge.

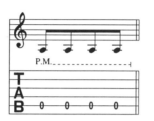

RAKE: Drag the pick across the strings indicated with a single motion.

TREMOLO PICKING: The note is picked as rapidly and continuously as possible.

ARPEGGIATE: Play the notes of the chord indicated by quickly rolling them from bottom to top.

VIBRATO BAR DIVE AND RETURN: The pitch of the note or chord is dropped a specified number of steps (in rhythm) then returned to the original pitch.

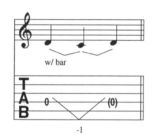

VIBRATO BAR SCOOP: Depress the bar just before striking the note, then quickly release the bar.

VIBRATO BAR DIP: Strike the note and then immediately drop a specified number of steps, then release back to the original pitch.

Additional Musical Definitions

 (accent) • Accentuate note (play it louder)

 (accent) • Accentuate note with great intensity

 (staccato) • Play the note short

⊓ • Downstroke

∨ • Upstroke

D.S. al Coda • Go back to the sign (𝄋), then play until the measure marked "***To Coda***," then skip to the section labelled "***Coda***."

D.S. al Fine • Go back to the beginning of the song and play until the measure marked "***Fine***" (end).

Rhy. Fig. • Label used to recall a recurring accompaniment pattern (usually chordal).

Riff • Label used to recall composed, melodic lines (usually single notes) which recur.

Fill • Label used to identify a brief melodic figure which is to be inserted into the arrangement.

Rhy. Fill • A chordal version of a Fill.

tacet • Instrument is silent (drops out).

 • Repeat measures between signs.

|1. |2. | • When a repeated section has different endings, play the first ending only the first time and the second ending only the second time.

NOTE: Tablature numbers in parentheses mean:
1. The note is being sustained over a system (note in standard notation is tied), or
2. The note is sustained, but a new articulation (such as a hammer-on, pull-off, slide or vibrato begins, or
3. The note is a barely audible "ghost" note (note in standard notation is also in parentheses).

Your Favorite Music For Guitar Made Easy

American Folksongs for Easy Guitar

Over 70 songs, including: All The Pretty Little Horses • Animal Fair • Aura Lee • Billy Boy • Buffalo Gals (Won't You Come Out Tonight) • Bury Me Not On The Lone Prairie • Camptown Races • (Oh, My Darling) Clementine • (I Wish I Was In) Dixie • The Drunken Sailor • Franky And Johnny • Home On The Range • Hush, Little Baby • I've Been Working On The Railroad • Jacob's Ladder • John Henry • My Old Kentucky Home • She'll Be Comin' Round The Mountain • Shenandoah • Simple Gifts • Swing Low, Sweet Chariot • The Wabash Cannon Ball • When Johnny Comes Marching Home • and more!
00702031 ....$12.95

The Big Christmas Collection

An outstanding collection of 100 Christmas tunes that even beginners can enjoy. Songs include: Away In A Manger • The Chipmunk Song • Deck The Hall • Feliz Navidad • Frosty The Snow Man • Fum, Fum, Fum • Grandma's Killer Fruitcake • Happy Holiday • It's Beginning To Look Like Christmas • Rudolph, The Red-Nosed Reindeer • Silent Night • Silver Bells • You're All I Want For Christmas • and more.
00698978....................................$16.95

The Broadway Book

Over 100 favorite show tunes including: All I Ask Of You • Beauty And The Beast • Cabaret • Edelweiss • I Whistle A Happy Tune • Memory • One • People • Sound Of Music • Tomorrow • With One Look • and more.
00702015 ...$17.95

The Big Book of Children's Songs

Over 60 songs, including: Are You Sleeping • The Bare Necessities • Beauty And The Beast • The Brady Bunch • The Candy Man • Casper The Friendly Ghost • Edelweiss • Feed The Birds • (Meet) The Flintstones • Happy Trails • Heigh Ho • I'm Popeye The Sailor Man • Jesus Loves Me • The Muffin Man • On Top Of Spaghetti • Puff The Magic Dragon • A Spoonful Of Sugar • Zip-A-Dee-Doo-Dah • and more.
00702027 ....$9.95

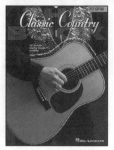

The Classic Country Book

Over 100 favorite country hits including: Another Somebody Done Somebody Wrong Song • Could I Have This Dance • Don't It Make My Brown Eyes Blue • Elvira • Folsom Prison Blues • The Gambler • Heartaches By The Number • I Fall To Pieces • Kiss An Angel Good Mornin' • Lucille • The Most Beautiful Girl In The World • Oh, Lonesome Me • Rocky Top • Sixteen Tons • Tumbling Tumbleweeds • Will The Circle Be Unbroken • You Needed Me • and more.
00702018....................................$19.95

The Classic Rock Book

89 monumental songs from the '60's, '70's and '80's, such as: American Woman • Born To Be Wild • Cocaine • Dust In The Wind • Fly Like An Eagle • Gimme Three Steps • I Can See For Miles • Layla • Magic Carpet Ride • Reelin' In The Years • Sweet Home Alabama • Tumbling Dice • Walk This Way • You Really Got Me • and more.
00698977....................................$19.95

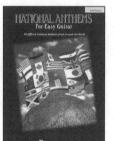

National Anthems For Easy Guitar

50 official national anthems in their original language, complete with strum and pick patterns and chord frames. Countries represented include Australia, Brazil, Canada, Cuba, France, Germany, Great Britain, Haiti, Irish Republic, Mexico, Peru, Poland, Russia, Sweden, United States of America, and more.
00702025 ....$12.95

The New Country Hits Book

100 hot country hits including: Achy Breaky Heart • Ain't Going Down ('Til The Sun Comes Up) • Blame It On Your Heart • Boot Scootin' Boogie • Chattahoochee • Don't Rock The Jukebox • Friends In Low Places • Honky Tonk Attitude • I Feel Lucky • I Take My Chances • Little Less Talk And A Lot More Action • Mercury Blues • One More Last Chance • Somewhere In My Broken Heart • T-R-O-U-B-L-E • The Whiskey Ain't Workin' • and more.
00702017....................................$19.95

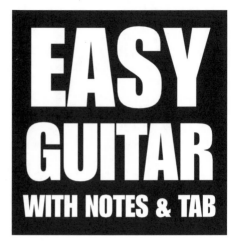

EASY GUITAR
WITH NOTES & TAB

This series features simplified arrangements with notes, TAB, chord charts, and strum and pick patterns.

00702026	90s Rock For Easy Guitar	$12.95
00702002	Acoustic Rock Hits	$12.95
00702001	Best of Aerosmith	$12.95
00702040	Best of Allman Brothers	$8.95
00702043	Best of Johnny Cash	$8.95
00702033	Best Of Steven Curtis Chapman	$12.95
00702028	Christmas Classics	$7.95
00702090	Eric Clapton's Best	$9.95
00702086	Eric Clapton – Live Acoustic	$10.95
00702048	Christmas Cheer	$10.95
00702016	Classic Blues For Easy Guitar	$12.95
00702053	Best of Patsy Cline	$8.95
00702006	Contemporary Christian Favorites	$9.95
00702091	Contemporary Country Ballads	$9.95
00702089	Contemporary Country Pickin'	$9.95
00702065	Contemporary Women of Country	$9.95
00702084	Best Of Def Leppard	$12.95
00702085	Disney Movie Hits	$9.95
00702041	Favorite Hymns	$9.95
00702057	Golden Age of Rock	$8.95
00699374	Gospel Favorites	$14.95
00702050	Great Classical Themes	$6.95
00702066	Great Hits of 1996-1997	$8.95
00699394	Guitar Wedding Collection	$14.95
00702037	Hits of the '50s	$10.95
00702035	Hits of the '60s	$10.95
00702046	Hits of the '70s	$10.95
00702047	Hits of the '80s	$8.95
00702054	Best of Hootie and the Blowfish	$9.95

00702059	Disney's The Hunchback of Notre Dame	$10.95
00702032	International Songs	$12.95
00702045	Jailhouse Rock, Kansas City and Other Hits by Leiber & Stoller	$8.95
00702021	Jazz Standards	$14.95
00702051	Jock Rock	$8.95
00702087	New Best Of Billy Joel	$9.95
00702088	New Best Of Elton John	$9.95
00702011	Best Of Carole King	$12.95
00702003	Kiss For Easy Guitar	$9.95
00699003	Lion King & Pocahontas	$9.95
00702005	Best Of Andrew Lloyd Webber	$10.95
00702061	Love Songs of the 50s & 60s	$8.95
00702062	Love Songs of the 70s & 80s	$8.95
00702063	Love Songs of the 90s	$9.95
00702052	Alanis Morissette – Jagged Little Pill	$10.95
00702039	Movie Themes	$10.95
00702067	The Nutcracker Suite	$5.95
00702030	Best Of Roy Orbison	$12.95
00702004	Rockin' Elvis	$9.95
00699415	Best Of Queen	$12.95
00702093	Rolling Stones Collection	$17.95
00702092	Best Of The Rolling Stones	$9.95
00702010	Best Of Rod Stewart	$12.95
00702049	Best Of George Strait	$10.95
00702042	Today's Christian Favorites	$8.95
00702029	Top Hits Of '95-'96 For Easy Guitar	$12.95
00702034	Top Hits Of '96-'97 For Easy Guitar	$12.95
00702007	TV Tunes For Guitar	$12.95

0198